gourd musical instruments

jim widess
ginger summit

Gourd Musical Instruments

Written and Produced by: Ginger Summit and Jim Widess
Project Director: Jim Widess
Engineer: Rob Sherman
Editor: Arthur Stephens
CD artwork: Elisha Couchman
Book Design: Andrea DuFlon
Photography: Jim Widess

Published by
The Caning Shop
926 Gilman St., Berkeley, CA 94710-1494
Phone: 1.800.544.3373
Fax: 1.510.527.7718
Email: gourdmusic@caning.com
http://www.caning.com
ISBN 0-9700338-0-X

Cover photo and drums by Jerraldine Hansen.
Printed in Hong Kong

today's Western orchestra contains instruments of sophistication and beauty. Centuries of adapting, testing and perfecting have produced acoustic musical organs whose sound is unsurpassed. For most of us, constructing one of these instruments is well beyond our capabilities and our skills. But all of these instruments are rooted in a much simpler past. When skills were less technical and tools were less exact. When nature provided the most essential part of the instrument—the gourd resonator.

The gourd, a close cousin to the pumpkin and zucchini, is a squash with an extremely hard shell. Closely associated with humans for over 11,000 years, it is one of the earliest natural containers. The qualities of the shell of the gourd made it very suitable for carrying food and liquids as well as providing a natural resonating chamber for rattles, rasps and drums.

For most instruments, the majority of the work in construction is centered around building the box, or the resonator. Gourds, being natural resonators, only require that they be cut open and cleaned. Presto! You have a banjo body, a drum frame, a bell for a wind instrument or a hollow tube for a flute.

In the forty-five tracks which follow are examples of forty different musical instruments—all made with gourds. All of these instruments are simple to build and require only very modest hand tools—ones you already are likely to own. You will be amazed at the variety of instruments you'll hear, as well as surprised by the quality of their sound.

Gourd resonator for berimbau with woodburned scene of a Capoeira event. Artwork by Oscar Baeza Woodburned gourd showing scenes of Capoeira by Eric Holder (Pirulito). Photo by Claire Garoutte.

berimbau

he berimbau, or musical bow, is an instrument that is associated with Brazil, but has its origins in East Africa, probably in the area of Angola to Swaziland. It was introduced to the Western Hemisphere by slaves who brought with them instruments and musical traditions from throughout Africa.

In Brazil, the berimbau is a very popular instrument which almost always accompanies *Capoeira*, a martial arts dance that evolved from slave games in the market place in the seventeenth and eighteenth centuries.

A good berimbau is made from a particularly strong yet flexible wood, usually *beriba* or ash. Originally the string was made from plant or animal materials, while now, the traditional string is made from wire material stripped from automobile tires, although medium gauge piano wire is also suitable. A gourd bowl is carefully selected to fit snugly against the outer curve of the bow, and secured by means of a string loop which firmly grips both the bow and the metal string.

A coin or stone is pinched between the thumb and forefinger of the hand supporting the bow. By pushing it hard against the string being tapped, different pitches can be created. The berimbau can be played by plucking or strumming with the fingers, but it is most often struck with a chopstick-like, small stick which is strong, flexible and straight with one end wrapped with string to provide a secure grip while playing.

The berimbau musician can produce distinctive rhythms that are easily distinguished by the *Capoeira* participants and the audience. Some are identified with specific schools or *maestres*, and others are associated with particular patterns of movement. While the instrument is most commonly associated with *Capoeira*, it can also be played as a solo instrument or with an orchestra or band playing samba or other popular music.

Track 1: "Iuna" Berimbau trio performed by Salih A. Qawi (Agua Seca), Marcelo Pereira (Capoeira Mandinga, PO Box 13502, Berkeley, CA 94712-4502), and Rene Macay (Escola Nova de Samba and Capoiera Mandinga). 0:32 (72)

Balafon, rattle, mvet (harp), bass
kalimba. Artwork by Arthur Stephens.
Photograph by Arthur Stephens

6

richmond indigenous gourd orchestra

he Richmond Indigenous Gourd Orchestra was formed in the 1980s by a group of ten musicians led by Arthur Stephens. While they each play traditional instruments, they were also intrigued by the unusual sounds in music from Africa and South America, and began to experiment with other sound sources. The gourd literally called to them in this search, and Stephens started growing gourds to create a wide variety of new instruments. Although they began by reproducing the familiar gourd instruments from both Africa and Brazil, the group usually added their own special twist, either in the instrument design and construction, the way it is played, or the way the sounds are amplified.

Most of the music played by the Richmond Indigenous Gourd Orchestra is original. One of the members may specifically compose a piece which is inspired by music from another culture. Or the pieces may simply evolve from group participation as they are playing together. Either way, each performance is filled with harmony, energy, and great enthusiasm.

All the instruments played by the group are constructed of gourds. These include a flute, a five-string harp, two sizes of lute, four different styles of mbira (including the bass kalimba), the friction drum (or cuica), the raspa (or guiro), a musical bow (similar to the berimbau) and several sizes of drum. A particularly interesting adaptation of the xylophone features gourd resonators suspended from a sturdy wooden frame. Different sets of keys can be laid across the top of the frame, thus producing a wide range of pitches with a single instrument.

In this selection, one prominent instrument is the bass kalimba. It is similar to the kalimba of West Africa, with a soundboard secured to a gourd bowl resonator. However, the keys are formed from hacksaw blades, and produce a deep resonating tone.

The cuica, or friction drum, also produces a distinctive sound at the end of the piece. It is similar to an open drum, with a cord attached to the center of the membrane. This cord can be plucked or rubbed to produce a distinctive low, guttural, percussive accent.

Track 2: balafon, bass kalimba, drums, mbira, rattles "Kundalini Calabash" from *Refuge in a Gourd*, track 3. ©1997, Richmond Indigenous Gourd Orchestra, PO Box 6561, Richmond, VA 23230. 5:36

Three Shekeres used on this track.

shekere

the shekere is a rattle with the noisemakers strung onto a netting that surrounds the outside of the gourd. While it is a very popular instrument throughout Africa, it is also very common in the Caribbean, Central and South America. The shekere is often used to accompany chants, songs, drums and dancing.

The shekere can be made with any size gourd, ranging from small rattles 4 inches in diameter to large gourds up to 18–24 inches in diameter. The netting is usually made of a flexible string or cord into which are tied beads, shells, pods or even buttons. The size and shape of the gourd, and the type of noisemaker, greatly affect the sounds created. When played, the player will often thump the bottom of the shekere in time producing a drum-like sound. Three shekeres are played in this selection. They are covered with glass beads which tend to create a sharper sound than other noisemakers.

This track is a traditional song to one of the gods played during the Santeria ceremonies in Cuba. The 6/8 rhythm is frequently used in this Afro-Cuban style.

Track 3: "Song to Ogun" Song to the god of iron in the Santeria religion. Afro-Cuban style. Shekere Trio performed by Orlando Hernandez, Russell Landers, Abdi Rashid Jibril. 1:50 (32)

Balafon player from Burkina Faso.
Photograph by Ginger Summit

balafon

the term 'balafon' refers to the African xylophone in which gourd resonators are suspended beneath each key. This type of instrument is very popular throughout Africa, and was brought to the Western Hemisphere by the slaves in the sixteenth century. Many variations of the instrument are found throughout the Caribbean, Central and South America, all rooted in their African past.

According to tradition in West Africa, the instrument is played only by men who are part of a family of "griots" or musicians who specialize in specific instruments. The music is rarely written down, so young boys apprentice with parents or relatives from an early age to learn the traditional songs and music. Each player acquires an individual style while maintaining the traditions of the culture.

The size of the balafon can range from nine to twenty-six keys or more. The keys are carefully shaped from hardwood that is tempered in fire. They are tuned to a pentatonic or heptatonic scale, depending on the area and culture where they are being played. The pitch range may also vary depending on traditions. The gourd resonators are carefully matched to each key so that the optimum sound of the key is amplified. One or two holes drilled into each gourd and then covered with a spider egg casing (or cigarette paper or cow or pig gut) provides a characteristic buzzing which adds to the complexity of the music.

The style of balafon most popular in West Africa has a somewhat flexible framework that is curved upwards at each end. A brace allows the player to carry the instrument while walking, although more frequently the instrument remains on the ground in front of the player.

Originally tradition dictated the times and events when the balafon could be played. In some locales the instrument is considered sacred and may only be played at funerals. In most places today, however, this instrument can be enjoyed by everyone in celebrations and gatherings of any occasion.

Track 4: Xylophone from Senegal with gourd resonators. Performed by Boynarr Sow. Boynarr performs with Sasso Barro in Davis, CA 1:12 (48)

Nhut Bui playing the Dan bau during concert at Clarion Music, San Francisco. Detail of horn pick and carved horn stem at end of Dan bau. Notice the 5 small circular marks on the face of the Dan bau. These are the harmonic nodes where the side of the hand is placed to stop the string. The 5th mark is below the right hand which is stopping the string at that node.

dan bau

the dan bau is a single-string, stick zither from Vietnam. It consists of a long wooden box approximately 48 inches in length by 8 inches in width. A flexible bamboo or carved, oxen-horn stem extends upright from one end of the box, with a gourd resonator attached to the stem about 2 inches above the box. While originally a string made of silk was used, today a steel string is tied to the flexible stem, extending through the gourd, and attaching to a tuning peg at the far end of the resonator box.

The instrument rests flat on the floor or on a table in front of the seated musician. The player holds the upright, flexible stem with the left hand, with which to increase or decrease tension on the string. With the right he holds a bamboo or horn pick to pluck the string, while stopping the string with the side of his palm, at various vibration nodes.

The extensive range of this monochord instrument is achieved by understanding the physics of a vibrating string. By using the side of the palm of the right hand to 'stop' the string at its natural harmonic nodes, the player can realize notes an octave or two higher than the fundamental tone of the string. Harmonic fifths and thirds can also easily be plucked. The notes in between can be found by stretching or shortening the string with the flexible stem. The gourd resonator amplifies the higher notes when plucking the very short string. The larger box amplifies the lower notes.

According to ancient legend, a fairy devised this instrument for a blind woman, making its sound resemble a human voice. Once a popular instrument among street musicians, it became part of court music in the nineteenth century. After World War II, more musicians became skillful on the dan bau, playing it both solo and with other instruments. Modern music is now being composed for it as well, so that the dan bau is a familiar instrument in Vietnam.

Track 5: "Cay Truc Xinh" (Pretty Bamboo), a folk tune of Vietnam. Dan bau performance by Phong Nguyen. 2:11 (100)

Musician playing the Kse diev in Northern Cambodia. This instrument has ivory at both ends of the stick.

kse diev

he kse diev (pronounced "se-d'io"), also known as the 'phi-n nam tao,' is an ancient single-string, stick zither found in Cambodia, Thailand and Vietnam. Its origins can be traced to India from a type of veena over one thousand years old. The resonator is one half of a bottle gourd, with the closed end attached to a long wooden neck which curves upward at the far end. The single string of silk or wire extends the length of the neck, but it is encircled by the loop of cord which firmly attaches the gourd to the neck. The vibrations of the string are thus transmitted to the gourd resonator on the opposite side of the neck.

When playing, the musician holds the instrument so that the opening of the gourd is pressed against his bare chest. While the string is plucked, the gourd is moved on and off different areas of the chest, which changes the resonant qualities of the tone. Very often the musician is also singing, which further affects the resonance of the music. The single string is plucked with a pick on the fourth finger and a bare index finger, while the other hand 'stops' the string in mid-air to change the pitch and also to create overtones. The sounds produced are quite soft, even with the gourd and chest serving as resonators.

While the kse diev used to be popular accompaniment to songs and folktales, it has now largely been replaced by a lute which is much easier to play. Although there are many examples of this instrument in museums and private collections, very few musicians today have mastered this instrument and its musical traditions.

Track 6: "Phat Cheay," performed on Kse Diev by Khan Heuan from *The Music of Cambodia*, Volume 3 (P)1994 Celestial Harmonies, PO Box 30122, Tucson, AZ 85751. Email: celestial@harmonies.com website: www.harmonies.com 2:34 (100)

Banjo made by Clarke Buehling. Photo by Clarke Beuhling.

banjo

the earliest string instruments were created and played throughout Africa for thousands of years. Lute-type instruments were constructed of small gourd bodies and stick, or carved wood, necks, with strings made of gut or plied animal hair. In the sixteenth and seventeen centuries, these were brought to the Western Hemisphere by the slaves, along with many other musical instruments. Plantation owners banned or destroyed many of the instruments, such as drums, fearing that they might be used to incite rebellion. However, the banjos, or banjars, were allowed and encouraged, so that the foundation for a strong musical tradition was laid. They remained an instrument of the slaves until the early 1800s, when the minstrel shows became popular. These instruments originally were made of a round gourd, with a head of sheep or coon skin, and with strings of horsehair. Soon, however, the gourd body was replaced by shaped wood, and the rest of the instrument underwent many changes.

In recent years there has been a movement back to the sounds and feel of the original instruments constructed with the original materials. Gourd bodies are carved from thick-shell gourds, with sound holes in the sides to permit transmission of sound. The body is covered with cowhide, goatskin, or even synthetic drum membrane, depending on the instrument maker and the musician. The neck is carved of a single piece of wood, and tuning pegs are shaped from ebony or rosewood.

Some banjo makers permanently fasten the head to the gourd by means of tacks or nails. Others have designed stringing mechanisms by which the head can be tuned or tightened in the event of change in weather or humidity that may affect the tension of the membrane.

The sound produced by the gourd banjo has attracted a sizeable following in recent years. Many instrument makers now craft instruments using the older materials and techniques, part of a tradition that is distinctly American but grounded in African roots.

Track 7: "Hard Times Jig / Old Virginny Jig" from *Clarke Buehling, Out of His Gourd.* All gourd banjo designed, built and performed by Clarke Buehling, PO Box 744, Fayetteville, AR 72702-0744 1:45 (90)

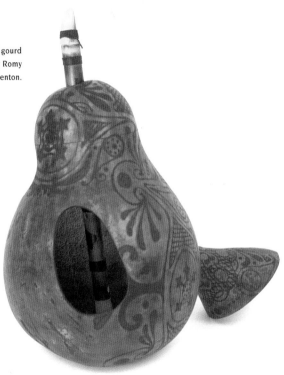

Bamboo clarinet and gourd resonator made by Romy Benton.

gourd resonator/clarinet

this clarinet made of bamboo, by Romy Benton, produces brilliant tones when played as a traditional instrument. But midway through this track he inserts the entire instrument into a large, hollow gourd to substantially alter the tone. The mouthpiece protrudes from one hole, and two larger holes on the sides of the gourd provide access for the hands. In this way, all of the tone has a secondary resonance through the gourd shell.

The effect is similar to the technique used by musicians of brass horns such as trumpet or trombone, who insert a mute made of plastic, metal or even small gourd into the bell. In both instances, the air is directed into a second chamber to modify the quality of sound.

Another instrument heard in this selection is the tamboura, a popular lute instrument played throughout India. The tamboura is a long-necked lute with up to four metal strings fastened to tuning pegs at the far end of the neck. It is used primarily to provide drone accompaniment either to voice, or within an ensemble of other instruments. While the body of the instrument may at one time have been made of a gourd (similar to the pierced lute of Persian ancestry), today most tamboura have bodies carved of jackwood.

Gourd drums also provide rhythm accompaniment in this selection.

Track 8: All gourd clarinet built and performed by Romy Benton. Tamboura and gourd drum. See Track 5. 1:11 (125)

Huluse photograph by
Randy Raine- Reusch.

hulu-se

this unusual instrument from Yunnan province of China is similar in style and configuration to the more familiar pungi or bin, the instrument of the snake charmers of India. A single gourd is used as the air reservoir, into which are inserted up to four pipes. However, in the hulu-se each pipe has a free reed made of silver or brass, mounted against an opening in the side near the upper end which is inserted into the gourd. One pipe with seven holes is used to play the melody. The other pipes provide the drones. One or more of these may be stopped with bits of wax to stop or alter the sound.

The sound of the traditional hulu-se is beautiful but soft, so that it is usually played alone rather than with other instruments. In China among the Dai people, it was commonly played by men in courtship or to serenade women. Now it is also played for recreation.

Information supplied by Randy Raine-Reusch.

Track 9: "Moon on Green Lake," Huluse Original composition by Randy Raine-Reusch. Box 1119n Stn A, Vancouver, BC Canada V6C 2T1. Email: rthree@sfu.ca—SOCAN 0:35 (126)

Sitar

sitar

t he sitar is a relatively recent variation of the veena, a stringed tube zither, that has been played in India for thousands of years. When it originally was introduced in the eighteenth century, the sitar had three strings, but gradually more strings were added so that now the instrument has seven strings and nineteen frets. The frets along the neck are arched metal pieces that allow for eleven or more sympathetic strings to be stretched immediately below the primary strings. The sitar has a main resonator body which is constructed of a gourd shell. An ornately carved wooden flare joins it to the neck. The top of the shell is usually closed with a thin veneer of jack wood. Attached to the opposite end of the neck is another gourd, or tumbra, which acts as a secondary resonator. The sitar is held across the chest with the body resting in the lap and the secondary resonator, over the shoulder.

The music of India is strictly governed by rules and traditions which are well known by everyone, including the audience. Historically, musical vibrations were thought to be connected to the spiritual world, so the ritual of the performance and the stability of the universe were intertwined. The main elements governing Indian music are the 'raga' or the basic melodic structure, and the 'tala,' or the cyclic measure of time. Both of these elements are defined and controlled by tradition, which musicians may take years to master. But within these strict guidelines the skillful musician may introduce his own improvisations.

A composition will generally begin with a very deliberate measured pace as the basic theme is introduced. Gradually the piece will develop in complexity and rhythm as the musician introduces his own improvisation.

The sitar may be played solo, as in this selection performed by Alan Perlman. But more usually, it is accompanied by the tabla, or pair of drums, and the tamboura, a stringed lute which provides a drone.

Track 10: "Yemen" Sitar Performed by Alan Perlman. Alan Perlman may be contacted at 1-415-242-4457 or arpmon@yahoo.com 2:22 (102)

Shekeres made by Orlando Hernandez.

shekere

the shekere is a very popular instrument used throughout Africa, the Caribbean, Central and South America. Because it is used in such a broad geographic and cultural spectrum, there are many variations in the way it is made, held, and played.

Shekeres range in size from small rattles held in one hand, to very large instruments up to 18–24 inches in diameter. Smaller instruments are usually held in one hand and shaken, struck against the thigh or hip, and tapped with the other hand. If the netting has a 'tail' made from the collected ends of the string net, the player may hold the ends with one hand and rhythmically "swish" or spin the gourd within the netting. The larger instrument is gently supported by the neck in one hand, while the other hand loosely supports and taps the bottom of the gourd. The shekere may be tossed from one hand to the other, shaken between the hands, or tossed and spun in the air.

While the shekere is almost always played as an accompaniment to other instruments, song, and dance, this solo piece composed and played by Orlando Hernandez demonstrates many of the various rhythms and sounds that can be produced. The drum-like thump comes from the player tapping the bottom of the gourd-shekere. Rhythms and types of sounds vary greatly, from Brazilian, Jamaican, Reggae, and the great variety of West African patterns. The shekere can have many voices in the hands of a master, from the loud and energetic pulsations to the gentle swish of beads against the gourd shell.

Track 11: Shekere Solo composed and performed by Orlando Hernandez. 2:16 (32)

'Ulili made by Nelson Ka'ai.

ʻulili

the ʻulili is a spinning rattle of Hawaii, usually played as a self-accompaniment for special hula dances or chants. This instrument was probably invented in Hawaii, and is rarely used today, except as a toy or in exhibition performances.

The ʻulili is made with three gourds which are pierced by a stick approximately 15 inches in length. The outer two gourds are secured firmly to the stick, with noisemakers of seeds, shells or pebbles inside. The center gourd has a hole through which a cord attached to the stick is threaded. The end of the cord is fastened to a knob or short stick as a handle.

To produce a sound, the string is wound on the stick inside the center gourd. The string is then pulled, causing the stick and outer gourds to spin. When the tension is released the string re-winds on the stick, similar to the action of a yo-yo, thus allowing a continuous sound to be produced.

One of the end gourds may also be tapped to provide additional percussion for the chant.

Hawaiian musical tradition emphasizes vocal elements, and percussion instruments such as the ʻulili always accompany chanting and dancing. The mele (chanted poetry) are usually directed to gods, ancestors, chiefs, and their descendants, and are considered sacred. Mele recount the historical and social foundations of the culture, and are carefully passed down from generation to generation.

Track 12: "Kaʻi Hoʻi" Hula ʻulili performed and chanted by Mahealani Uchiyama. ʻUlili by Nelson Kaʻai. Mahea Uchiyama Dance Theater, www.mahea.com 1:12 (27)

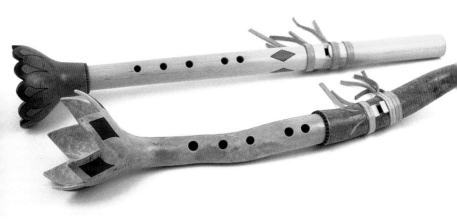

Bamboo slot flute with gourd bell and all gourd slot flute made by Cliff Walker.

slot flute

While there are many different types of flutes found throughout the world, this particular form was created and played primarily by the Indians of North America. Slot flutes were originally constructed of many different types of material, including bamboo, reeds, elderberry, ash and especially red cedar. It is also possible to make a slot flute out of the handle of a dipper gourd.

The flute consists of three main elements: the tube, a block that stops the airflow approximately one-third of the distance from the end of the tube, and a cover piece. When bamboo is used, one of the nodes forms a natural barrier, or block in the center of the tube. As the name implies, a slot or opening is carved in the side of the tube directly over the block or barrier. The edge of this slot, furthest from the front or mouthpiece of the flute, is carved to a sharp edge. A cover piece is cut from another piece of wood, with a narrow groove carved on its underside, and tied over the slot in such a way that air blown into the tube is directed over the block, through the groove, and against the sharp edge. This creates a vibrating column of air that is resonated through the length of the tube. Finger holes are made in the side of the tube to produce notes. Typical slot flutes are tuned to a pentatonic scale, although the exact tuning varies among tribes and individual players.

The slot flute was, and continues to be, a very important instrument among the native American Indians. The cover over the opening frequently is carved to represent the fetish or spirit protector of the musician. This instrument is often played along with the drum and rattle at rituals and ceremonies of the tribe.

Track 13: All gourd slot flute based on Native American reed flute. Traditional melody taken from "The Indians Book, Dover edition published 1968. Built and performed by Cliff Walker 1:15 (116)

Mbira and hosho rattles

mbira

the mbira is a type of lamellaphone, a large family of instruments found throughout Africa and much of Latin America, to which the music box is related. Common to all of the instruments in this family are a set of tines or tongues firmly mounted on a sound board, and a resonator. These pieces may be combined as a single unit (such as the kalimba) or separate as the mbira. This form of instrument is most beautifully developed in Zimbabwe, where the sound boards may hold from twelve to thirty-six tines. The sound board (made of carved hardwood) is then firmly wedged inside a large bowl-shaped resonator, or deze, which traditionally is a large gourd. To add complexity to the sounds produced, metal discs or shells are added either to the sound board or around the circumference of the resonator.

The different sizes and styles of keyboard, number, placement and order of keys, as well as the tunings vary depending on the particular village or musical traditions of the group.

The *mbira dzavadzimu* which is heard in this selection is most closely associated with communities in central Zimbabwe, usually played by a few recognized musicians for spiritual and ceremonial events. The sound of the instrument and the songs it accompanies are felt to create a link between the physical world and the world of the spirits.

The hosho rattles which are also heard in this selection are a frequent accompaniment to mbira music played by the Shona people. Although occasionally made of tin cans, traditional hosho rattles are made of the maranka gourd. The bulb of the maranka gourd typically has a wrinkled exterior shell. When grown on the ground, the stem end twists into a naturally curved handle. The gourd is thoroughly cleaned inside and out, and then noisemakers of seeds, beans, shells or pebbles are added. The hole can be plugged with a cork or sealed with woven fiber. Hosho are always played in pairs, providing a soft percussive sound to accompany the mbira.

Track 14: "*Shumba Huru*," "The Great Lion," *mbira dzavadzimu* in a *deze* (gourd resonator) with Hosho rattles. A traditional Shona (Zimbabwe) song for calling on the *mhondoro* (guardian spirits) for assistance with rain, crops, etc. Performed by Russ Landers and Sarah Noll. 1-510-763-1722, LanderNoll@aol.com Mbira (keyboard) maker: Tute W. Chigamba. 2:13 (23, 40)

Kora

kora

The kora is a twenty-one string plucked harp/lute played in West Africa in the area of The Gambia, Senegal, Mali, Burkina Faso and Ivory Coast. The term harp/lute is derived from the fact that it is shaped much like a lute with a very large, leather-covered, gourd resonator and a single long neck which passes through the resonator and extends approximately 2½ feet beyond. The strings are anchored on a metal ring at the far edge of the resonator and then are attached along the neck with turning collars of knotted leather. The twenty one nylon strings are arranged in two parallel lanes at right angles to the leather sounding surface. They pass through a vertical notched bridge, with eleven strings on the left and ten on the right. Two additional shorter wooden posts extend through the sound table parallel to the neck. These serve as handles which the musician grasps in his hands so as to leave the thumb and index finger free to pluck the strings.

In performance, the 'griot' (or 'jali' as kora musicians are known in West Africa) sits holding the kora nearly vertical in front of him with the base resting on the ground on in the lap. A rhythmic pattern may be added by a second player who strikes the back of the resonator with a thin stick or long needle. Singers may accompany the music with clapping, or by striking tuned metal bells.

The kora is a very important instrument in rituals, ceremonies and social gatherings. Traditionally the instrument can only be played by members of designated families. Because it is a difficult instrument to master, young boys are apprenticed to masters at an early age. They not only learn to play the instrument, but also learn the narrations and recitations which contain the history and cultural knowledge of the community. Virtuoso players are known for their distinctive technique, tunings and song style.

Today the kora is being integrated with contemporary instruments such as dance bands and popular musical groups.

Track 15: "Kelefaba" Kora. Performed by Alan Perlman. Alan Perlman may be contacted at 1-415-242-4457 or arpmon@yahoo.com 3:02 (82)

Gourd water drums made by Victor Mario Zaballa,
Arte Sintesis, San Francisco, CA

water drum

the gourd water drum makes use of the special sound-conducting qualities of water. A gourd bowl is inverted on top of water in a larger container, either a pail or large gourd. The smaller gourd may have a cord connected to one side of the rim, allowing it to be raised slightly by an assistant as it is being played. The beater is either a padded mallet or a gourd cup with handle.

The sound produced by the water drum is an interesting combination of the concussive knock of two hard objects, and the lower resonance of the water. Multiple pitches are produced by different size bowls inverted on the water. In this selection, musician Steve Cervantes uses a tray filled with water which is large enough to hold many different size gourd bowls. In this way he is able to produce a wide range of tones with this simple instrument.

This instrument originated in both Africa and Meso-America, where it is still used. In West Africa, it typically is played by women for their own ceremonies and festivities, informally constructed of materials which already exist in their households. The Indians in northern Mexico devised a similar instrument which is often played during rituals of planting and harvest. (see track 43)

Track 16: Gourd water drum, original pieces by Steve Luis Cervantes, http://www.multicultural-music.com 1-800-796-3047. 1:51 (19)

Berimbau and caxixi made by Agua Seca of
Mandingueiros da Capoeira.

caxixi and berimbau

the berimbau is the traditional instrument that accompanies the martial arts dance of *Capoeira* of Brazil. It most probably derived from the musical bow, an instrument found throughout sub-Sahara Africa, in which initially, the player used his mouth at the end of the stick as a resonator. A gourd is fastened to the bow and frequently a loop of string overlaps the wire string as well, dividing the string so as to create two fundamental tones. The gourd serves to provide resonance as the wire is struck by a bamboo stick. By pulsing the gourd against the chest or abdomen, the resonance can be muted to create distinctive sound variations. (see track 1)

When playing the berimbau, the musician traditionally holds a caxixi rattle by a loop around the middle fingers of the same hand that holds the stick. As he strikes the wire, he also shakes the caxixi, thus creating an additional percussion accompaniment to the berimbau. The caxixi consists of a basket container which has a gourd disc as a base, enclosing sound makers of seeds or pebbles. The top of the basket is closed and shaped to create a loop large enough for one or two fingers. Larger instruments of this style are played in West Africa as shakers or rattles to accompany drum ensembles.

A third instrument often used to accompany *Capoeira* is the *atabaque* (drum). In this selection it is easy to identify all three instruments.

Track 17: "Miudinho" Berimbau, caxixi (gourd basket rattle), and atabaque (drum). Performed by Salih A. Qawi (Agua Seca), Marcelo Pereira, (Capoiera Mandinga) and Rene Macay (Escola Nova de Samba and Capoiera Mandinga). 1:12 (72, 28)/

Steps in making an all
gourd didgeridoo
by Paul Sedgwick.

didgeridoo

the didgeridoo is an instrument of the Yolngu (Aborigine) people of Northern Australia. Traditionally it is made from the straight branches of eucalyptus trees approximately 6 feet in length that have been hollowed out by termites. The mouth-end of the hollow tube is fitted with a rim of beeswax to allow for a snug fit against the lips. Originally it was played by men in secret religious ceremonies, accompanied by tapping sticks, hand-clapping and singing. Today the instrument has been incorporated in many musical traditions, from jazz to popular songs, and by all manner of musical groups.

Paul Sedgwick makes a didgeridoo by joining several straight snake gourds with glue and wood dough. Because the shells of snake gourds are frequently very thin, Sedgwick adds weight and strength by leaving some of the pulp attached to the walls, and then coating the entire surface with Bond-O resin.

The instrument is played by blowing into the opening through loosely vibrating lips which produces a fundamental note. In order to create a continuous tone of constant pitch, circular breathing is used. (Frequent small breaths of air breathed in from the nose are stored in the cheeks, and then blown out through the lips in a constant stream.) This technique requires great control, and boys in Australia are given instruction from an early age. Virtuoso players are identified by the wide variety of techniques that can be used to create overtones, superimpose rhythmic patterns, and add different voiced sounds such as croaking or gurgling to imitate animal sounds.

The player may sit or stand while performing. Occasionally he may move around with the singers and dancers. The more usual style, however, is to sit with the far end of the tube rested on the foot.

Track 18: all gourd Didgeridoo Paul Sedgwick 1:51 (119)

Bamboo didgeridoo
with gourd resonator
made by
Romy Benton.

didgeridoo

this didgeridoo was constructed by Romy Benton of bamboo. The inner surface of bamboo is usually very dense and does not require further sealant. However, occasionally Benton will coat the inner surface with a wood sealant to provide additional resonance.

Frequently, traditional didgeridoo players will set the end of the instrument within a shell or tin container to provide additional resonance. Benton adapted this technique by permanently affixing a gourd bell to the bottom of the bamboo tube.

In this selection, he combines the haunting drone sounds of the didgeridoo with other instruments from Africa (gourd drums), Latin America (caxixi rattles—see track 17) and China (hulu-se —see Track 9). Combining instruments from around the world creates unique sounds quite popular in today's world where cultures mix and share traditions. Each instrument can be readily identified, but working together they create a piece of unusual complexity.

Track 19: Didgeridoo with gourd resonator, Huluse, drum and caxixi, performed by Romy Benton. Didgeridoo handmade by Romy Benton. From *Wind in the Grass* track 8. ©1998 Grasswind Records, Portland, OR. Romy@teleport.com. Romy Benton, PO Box 10871, Portland, OR 97296. 2:35 (28, 119, 126)

Snake charmer in India with gourd pongi. Photo by Jane
Woolverton. Closeup of gourd pongi or bin (facing page).

bin/pungi

the snake charmer playing his flute to lure cobras out of their baskets is a popular sight in India. The pipe which is used is very old, and has many different names and forms: pungi, tiktiri, and been or bin.

The instrument consists of a small gourd which serves as an air reservoir. In the base of the bulb are inserted two reed or bamboo pipes. The pipes each have a single beating reed which is activated when the musician blows into the stem end of the gourd and the air passes through the tubes. The beating reeds are usually formed from a very thin slice of the bamboo pipe's skin, although occasionally thin metal is used instead.

One of the pipes has a single hole enabling it to produce one tone, or a drone. The other pipe has several holes on which a melody is played. To maintain a continuous tone, the musician must use a circular breathing technique (similar to that used to play the didgeridoo).

(A familiar adaptation of this instrument in Europe is recognized as the bagpipe of Scotland. The musician blows into the air reservoir, and applying even pressure on the bag by squeezing with the arm, a steady tone is maintained. This is much simpler than trying to master the circular breathing technique.)

Since snakes are deaf, cobras do not respond to the sound of the snake charmer. More likely, they are responding to the snake charmer's undulating movement as well as the cobra-like profile of the gourd flute in the swaying flute-players hands.

The unusual, nasal quality of the idioglottal reed of the bin, can be an exciting addition to a modern band.

Track 20: "Sawar," Bin. Original composition by Randy Raine-Reusch. Box 1119n Stn A, Vancouver, BC Canada V6C 2T1. Email: rthree@sfu.ca—SOCAN 1:07 (120)
Track 21: Bin. "Reed Gourd Voices" Original composition and performed by Darrell Davore, a musician for life with 32 years of instrument making and sound art "experience." 1:11 (120)

Different configurations of traditional gourd pigeon flutes from China. Gourd pigeon flute in position on homing pigeon.

gourd pigeon flutes

igeon flutes can be traced back to the twelfth Century in China. If you think of homing pigeons as the earliest form of tele-communication, then the pigeon flute was the earliest alert for "you've got mail!" In early literature the sound of a flock of pigeons with their flutes was referred to as "heavenly music."

Four different configurations of the gourd flutes which are usually made are "Gourd whistle," "Star-surrounding-the-moon whistle," "seven-star whistle," and "eleven-eye whistle." These four styles are also made with three different sized gourds which have deeper or higher tones depending on the size of the gourd and pipes.

The gourd is cut open, and a cap of bamboo or bone is made to fit the opening. Into the cap is cut a slit which the wind enters to create the turbulence. The size of the gourd and its pipes, determines the tones. Frequently the gourd bowl is divided into two chambers by means of a partition. The chambers, being unequal in size, produce two distinct tones which harmonize. They are augmented with thin, bamboo-veneer pipes which produce higher tones in harmony with the tones from the gourd.

The entire flute is very light and attaches to the rump of the pigeon. The middle tail feathers are tied or sewn together first, very close to the rump, and then again about ½ inch out from the rump. A small bone tang glued and pinned to the bottom of the flute, slides through the slit that has been tied off. A metal ring is slipped through a hole in the tang, below the tail feathers, locking the flute into place. The gourd rests on the rump so that as the bird flies, the wind is directed to the slits in the gourd top.

With a great clapping of hands, the first bird takes flight and the flute begins to sound. As it circles overhead, there is another flapping of wings and the second bird takes flight. As more birds join the flock, the sound intensifies. See if you can hear each bird take flight and then join the flute chorus as they continue to circle overhead in a flock.

Track 22: Seven Pigeons flying with mounted gourd flutes. Old Chinese Gourd Flutes courtesy of Steve Klausner, Dove's Flight, Glen Ellen, CA. Pigeons courtesy of Don Dickinson, Martinez, CA. 1:47 (130)

Detail of kite with array of large
and small gourd whistles.
Photograph © Pierre Fabre.
Nantong Kite in flight.
Photograph © Pierre Fabre.
Detail of kite flute tied
onto kite (facing page).
Photo by Uli Wahl.

kite flutes

Sound instruments have been attached to kites in China since the tenth Century. With the development of the pigeon flute, similar gourd flutes have been used on kites. Since the kite is so much larger than a pigeon and weight is not as critical of an issue, many single-toned gourd flutes, rather than multi-toned flutes, are added. In some cases over 100 gourd flutes, some quite large, might be found on a single, giant kite.

The construction of kite flutes is generally the same as with the central gourd pigeon flute, with the cap being carved from bamboo, ebony, or bone.

The laminar air flow, which keeps the kite aloft, speeding down the face of the kite strikes the edge of the slot on the tops of the gourds, causing them all to sound.

Track 23: Kite Flute made by Uli Wahl The flutes are fixed on the windward surface of a kite. At heights of several hundred meters, the speeding wind makes the flutes' sound audible at a distance of 500 meters. Uli Wahl, Domhofgasse 21, 69469 Weinheim, Germany. http://members.aol.dom/woinem1/index/index.htm 0:51 (132)

Track 24: Kite Flute made by Uli Wahl http://members.aol.dom/woinem1/index/index.htm 0:17 (132)

Combination gourd rainstick and shekere made by Daniel Randolph and Hede Cult.

rainstick

this instrument, which is very popular today among percussionists, has been used for hundreds of years by Indians in Meso-America and South America, primarily within cultures that relied on agriculture for sustenance. The traditional name is *chica huastli*, or rattling stick. Early documentation dating from the 1500s indicates that it was used in rituals in villages prior to planting, asking the spirits to cleanse the earth prior to planting.

There are many forms of rainstick. It can be made of bamboo, hollowed branches, carved wood, as well as thoroughly cleaned gourds. Some images found in Mayan carvings depict a stick up to eight feet in length with a bulb at one end held above the head of the musician. It is possible that a gourd was attached to one end of a hollow stick to hold the sound-makers, although a long-handled dipper gourd with a thick handle could also be used for this purpose. Thorns, or more recently bamboo skewers, are inserted into the sides of the hollow tube in clockwise spirals for the entire length. Before sealing the container, sound-makers are added. Huichol indians of Mexico require that these sound-makers be stones selected for a source of water, that is smooth pea-sized pebbles from a stream or ocean.

The rainstick is still used in many Huichol ceremonies. A version made of a long bamboo tube is played by men, while rounded bottle gourd containers are used by the women. In some rituals, the rainstick is used only by the shaman to announce his entrance to the site of the ceremony.

Some ancient depictions of rainsticks are elaborately decorated with images of intertwined serpents or with Tlaloc, the god of rain. Today rainsticks are more often left plain or embellished only with strips of ribbon or leather and beads.

Track 25: All gourd rainstick designed and built by Daniel Randolph and Hedy Cult. Performed by Orlando Hernandez. 0:44 (30)

BBs are added to the gourd Ocean Drum, invented by
Xavier Quijas Yxayotl, American Indigena.

mayan ocean drum

he Mayan ocean drum may be considered a novelty instrument now, but many hundreds of years ago it was an important instrument in rituals of Indians in Mexico, primarily among coastal Mayan communities. It was played during events that were designed to honor the spirits of the ocean, to pay tribute for the fish on which the community depended. In addition, the ceremony most likely was intended to ask that lives be spared, since small canoes on the ocean always presented high risks.

The drum originally was a hollow turtle shell, bowl of wood or gourd shell in which round pebbles were rolled around the inside surface. A later innovation added a membrane to enclose the container. This greatly increased the resonance, especially when the container was turned over and the pebbles rolled on the inner surface of the taut membrane.

While the pebbles originally were small stones from beach or riverbed, rounded semi-precious stone such as jade, jadite, turquoise and alabaster gave added significance to the instrument and the sounds which it produced.

The Mayan ocean drum was reinvented by Xavier Quijas Yxayotl in 1978.

Track 26: Ocean Drum made by Xavier Quijas Yxayotl., 1044 S Gage Ave, Los Angeles, CA 90023 Performed by Jim Widess. 1:02

Ipu heke

ipu heke

the ipu heke is a traditional Hawaiian gourd instrument and is played by musicians to accompany hula and chants. Early lithographs dating from the 1700s show the instrument being played in ceremonies, and this instrument seems to be unique to Hawaii. The ipu heke heard on this track is constructed of two gourds which are cleaned and then trimmed to join together to form one hour-glass shape. A cord is securely wrapped around the join. Although this instrument is commonly called a drum, no membrane is involved in its construction, so the ipu is technically not a drum but an idiophone.

When played by a skilled musician, the instrument is capable of producing many distinct sounds, depending on where or how the gourd shell is struck. The chanter/drummer kneels on the ground in front of a mat or pad. The drum is lifted by the cord handle and thumped on the pad, producing a deep resonating tone. The shell is then lifted and struck with the heel of the hand on the base of the drum. By tapping the sides of the shell with the fingers, still another sound is produced.

A similar smaller instrument (ipu heke 'ole) is made by cutting the top off a bottle gourd and wrapping a cord around the narrow waist. This smaller instrument is often played by dancers as well as kneeling musicians.

As ancient traditions are being revived, use of the ipu heke continues to be popular in Hawaii. Because gourds have different resonating characteristics, each musician specifically selects the gourds of his/her own instrument, and maintains it for exclusive, personal use.

Track 27: "HuaKa'i Hele" Ipu heke. "Pa'i" drumming and "Mele" chant by Mahealani Uchiyama. Ipu heke made by Kimo. Mahea Uchiyama Dance Theater, www.mahea.com 2:08 (20)

Winston Ka'uhane Morton playing tear drop ipu hokiokio (nose flute), made by B Ka'imiloa Chrisman, MD. Detail of tear drop ipu hokiokio (nose flute), made by B Ka'imiloa Chrisman, MD.

nose flute

the tradition of flutes played by breathing through the nose may seem unusual, but this form of playing is very familiar in many cultures around the world, particularly among the islands of Oceania from Tahiti to the Philippines. It is commonly thought that air breathed through the nose is cleaner, and therefore purer, than air breathed through the mouth.

Most nose flutes are made of hollowed wood, bone or bamboo. But in Hawaii these flutes were also made with a small pear-shaped gourd, hence the name 'tear-drop flute.' The instrument has one opening near the stem end, and two or three finger holes arranged in a horizontal row along one side, allowing for several notes to be produced.

Gourd nose flutes are frequently referred to as lovers whistles as they were used by young people to communicate during courtship. The nose flute has also been used as an accompaniment to chants, along with the ipu-heke, or drum.

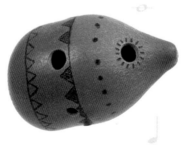

Track 28: Tear drop Nose Flute made by B. Ka'imiloa Chrisman, M.D. Original composition, performed by Winston Ka'uhane Morton 0:15 (132)

Track 29: Slightly smaller nose flute than Track 28 made by B. Ka'imiloa Chrisman, M.D. , Original composition, performed by Winston Ka'uhane Morton 0:12 (132)

richmond indigenous gourd orchestra

this group of five to ten imaginative musicians creates all their instruments out of gourds to produce an unusual but fascinating blend of sounds and rhythms. (See the description for track 2.)

In addition to the instruments described in their previous track, two other instruments can be heard in this selection: the flute and the water drum.

The flute is constructed from the handle of a dipper gourd and has five finger holes. It is side-blown, like a fife or transverse flute . By coating the interior of the tube with varnish, the instrument produces a sparkling tone.

The water-drum is created by overturning gourd bowls on water in larger tubs. The gourds are then struck by a soft mallet to produce a sound that resonates through the water. Multiple tones are created by using several size bowls on the water (see track 16 for further information).

Several different rattles can also be heard. These include rattles of many sizes, some with the noisemakers placed inside the gourd before sealing the opening with the handle. Others have nets surrounding the gourd which are imbedded with noisemakers, similar to the shekere. Each type of rattle produces a very distinctive sound.

Track 30: Balafon, drum, rattles, flute, water-drum, Performed by the Richmond Indigenous Gourd Orchestra. From *Refuge in a Gourd*, track 5, "Dance of the Pollinators." ©1997, Richmond Indigenous Gourd Orchestra, PO Box 6561, Richmond, VA 23230. 4:18 (19, 48, 52, 114)

A performance of Venancio Notico Mbande's timbila orchestra. Photo by Andrew Tracey.

chopi xylophone orchestra

the instruments being played on this track are very closely related to the balafon of West Africa. However, the Chopi of southern Africa have introduced many refinements to create a very different sound and this variation of xylophone is called "mbila" or "timbila." The timbila consist of up to nineteen keys made of a hard, heavy, resinous wood that has been fire tempered to improve resonance. Unlike the balafon, which has a lightweight frame that is often carried by a circular brace while the musician is walking, the timbila has a much heavier framework, the base of which is a single piece of wood with holes along its length. Fastened to the underside of the holes are graduated, gourd resonators matched to the keys set on top of the frame. The gourd is firmly sealed to the framework with wax. A hole made in the side of each gourd resonator is covered with a fine membrane of animal intestine and then protected by an additional ring of gourd attached to the side of the gourd; this addition creates a buzzing tone when the key above the resonator is struck.

The timbila keys are tuned to a heptatonic scale, and the instruments are made in several pitch ranges. While most have from ten to fifteen keys, the base timbila has only four keys and provides a continuous drone accompaniment for the other instruments.

Before Mozambique gained independence, every chief in that area had his own timbila orchestra. Today, however, the timbila orchestras of ten to twenty instruments are familiar entertainment at most public and private gatherings, including dances, in south-east Africa. The music follows traditional patterns of rhythm and melody, yet each player still performs with his own style, which combines to create a very complex music.

Track 31: "Chibhudhu" Chopi xylophone orchestra. Composed and built by Venancio Notico Mbande, master musician of the Chopi people, Inhambane district, southern Mozambique, composer, maker and leader in their 'timbila' orchestral xylophone tradition. Contact: ilat@giraffe.ru.ac.za Recorded by Curt Wittig. 1:56 (134)

Keluri. Photograph by Randy Raine- Reusch. Keluri being
played in procession. Photo by Randy Raine-Reusch

keluri

the keluri is a form of mouth organ related to the Chinese sheng made from a gourd and bamboo. The keluri and closely related enkulurai are found in Borneo: the keluri is used by the people in the 'upriver' or inland areas, and the enkulurai is played near the coast. Both instruments consist of a gourd wind chamber which supports six bamboo pipes. Each pipe has a free reed, constructed either of thinly sliced bamboo or metal which is embedded in the chamber of the gourd. The average length of the pipe is approximately two feet.

The instrument is played by holding the gourd between the two hands with the fingertips pointing upward to touch the holes in the side of each pipe. When the hole is closed by a finger, each pipe can produce one note. The low note of the longest tube is sounded continuously, much like a drone. With the remaining five notes the musician creates simple melodies. Because several pipes can be "closed" at the same time, harmonic chords can be played along with the melody line, by one player.

Both instruments were played for "long dances" that were associated with the rituals connected with headhunting. However, as this tradition ceased, the instruments also stopped being played. While some older members of the communities are able to play them, knowledge of these instruments will likely disappear.

Information supplied by Randy Raine-Reusch.

Track 32: "Malam Ulu," Keluri Original composition by Randy Raine-Reusch. Box 1119n Stn A, Vancouver, BC Canada V6C 2T1. Email: rthree@sfu.ca—SOCAN 1:42 (126)

Sumpotan Photograph by Randy Raine-Reusch

sumpotan

the sumpotan is another free reed instrument related to the Chinese sheng and the khaen of Thailand. It is found in Borneo and throughout Malaysia, where it is still a popular instrument, particularly among the Dusun people. It consists of a small, gourd air-chamber with a blowing hole at the stem end. Although there are eight bamboo pipes, only seven have free reeds. They are arranged in two rows, and extend through the gourd such that the bottom end of the pipe is exposed and open. Pitch is controlled by fingerholes at the sides of the pipes, although three of the pipes are also stopped by plugging the ends with the fingers. Two sets of three pipes are tuned to a major or minor chord, thus allowing chordal melodies to be played without special fingering.

Because the length of the pipes can extend up to three feet in length, they are often played with the pipes pointing sideways or down. The instrument may be played as a solo instrument for personal entertainment, or as part of a band with other local instruments.

Information supplied by Randy Raine Reusch.

Track 33: "Hijau Pucuk Pisang," Sumpotan Original composition by Randy Raine-Reusch. Box 1119n Stn A, Vancouver, BC Canada V6C 2T1 Email: rthree@sfu.ca—SOCAN 1:35 (126)

Naw Photograph by
Randy Raine- Reusch

naw

he naw, also known as a hulu-sheng, is the earliest form of the free reed instruments. Invented some 3000 years ago by the Chinese, it is found in the hill country of northern Thailand, Laos and Burma, where it is played by the Lahu and Lisu people. It consists of five bamboo pipes which are arranged in a circular pattern extending completely through a gourd air reservoir. The open ends of the pipes are trimmed flush with the surface of the gourd shell, allowing the player to 'bend' the notes by covering the ends of the pipe with his thumb while playing.

The bamboo free reeds are sealed inside the wind chest. A hole in the tube just above the surface of the gourd must be closed by the fingertips in order for the reed to sound. More recently, the reeds are made of hammered metal instead of the traditional bamboo.

This instrument was commonly used during courtship or for communication between unmarried people.

Information supplied by Randy Raine Reusch.

Track 34: Naw Traditional Lahu performance recorded by Randy Raine-Reusch, 1984 in Chiang Mai, Thailand. Randy Raine-Reusch. Box 1119n Stn A, Vancouver, BC Canada V6C 2T1 Email: rthree@sfu.ca—SOCAN. 1:08 (126)

Track 35: "Pasad Di," Naw. A traditional five pipe, gourd and bamboo free-reed mouth organ native to the Lahu and Lisu peoples of Northern Thailand. Original composition by Randy Raine-Ruesch. Box 1119n Stn A, Vancouver, BC Canada V6C 2T1 Email: rthree@sfu.ca—SOCAN 1:04 (126)

Gourd banjo by
Robert Thornburg

banjo

the fact that the American banjo is rooted in the African slave past is documented by many chroniclers of the early history of The United States:

"They have several sorts of Instruments in imitation of Lutes, made of small Gourds fitted with Necks, strung with Horse hairs, or the peeled stalks of climbing Plants or Withes. These Instruments are sometimes … covered with Parchment or other Skin wetted, having a Bow for its Neck, the Strings ty'd longer or shorter, as they would alter their sounds." Sir Hans Sloan, 1689, after a trip to Jamaica, describing a "strum-strum."

"… made from a half of a calabash covered with skin scraped like parchment, with a rather long neck. Four strings of silk or dried bird gut were raised on a bridge above the skin. It was played by plucking and beating on the strings." Jean Baptiste Labat, 1694, after a trip to Martinique.

"This musical instrument [banjo] is made of a Gourd something in the imitation of a Guitar, with only four strings and played with the fingers in the same manner." Nicholas Creswell, 1774, wrote in his journal in Maryland.

"The instrument proper to them is the Banjar, which they brought from Africa, and which is the original of the guitar, its chords being precisely the four lower chords of the guitar." Thomas Jefferson wrote in 1781, in a footnote.

All the above quotations from: Epstein, Dena J., "The Folk Banjo: A Documentary History," Ethnomusicology, Vol. XIX, Number 3, September, 1975.

Track 36: "Liza Jane." All gourd banjo built and performed by Robert Thornburg, Sierra View Acoustic Music, 1478 Rocking W Dr, Bishop, CA 93514. http://wmpub.com/gourdbjo.html gourdbanjo@aol.com 1:36 (90)

Bro of the Ede people.
Photograph by Ta Quang Dong

bro

the bro is similar to the kse diev (see track 6). It is also called the phin phia (or pin pia) in Northern Thailand, where it is native to the tribes in the Chiang Mai region, and the Jorai people of Vietnam. This type of instrument most likely originated in Northern India as a type of veena, or tube zither. A long wooden neck is connected to the closed end of a gourd, bowl-shaped resonator. Six raised frets are attached to the wooden neck allowing the musician to control the pitch of the strings. Two strings are anchored to both ends of the neck. At one end rings of cord or twine are used to adjust the tuning.

This instrument is often used by a singer as self-accompaniment in informal settings. Until recently it has been a popular instrument by young men to court girls. However, familiarity and skill in playing this instrument, like many others, is unfortunately becoming a lost art.

Track 37: "Improvisation" Bro. A two stringed zither. One string is fretted, the second acts as a drone. Performed by Dinh Van Bang in Hara Village, Gia Lai Province, Vietnam. Recorded by Phong Nguyen 1:00 (90)

Goong. Photograph
by Phong Nguyen

goong

this thirteen-string, bamboo and gourd tube zither is played by the Bahnar people of Pleiku province in Vietnam. Originally the strings were cut from the skin of the bamboo tube and carefully lifted by inserting short pieces of wood between the skin "strings" and the bamboo tube to tension them, as is done with bamboo raft zithers in Africa. Now these strings are metal. Since the tube is round and the strings from the skin of the tube went around the tube, the metal strings still follow this configuration. The strings are plucked in sequence, individually, or together as chords.

Track 38: "B'ru" (Tomb Festival) Goong. A bamboo zither with 2 large gourd resonators. Performed by M'piet, P'chak Village, Gia Lai Province, Vietnam. Recorded by Phong Nguyen. 0:39 (90)

Mr. Dieu Xrot playing the Mbuat.
Photograph by Phong Nguyen

mbuat

the mbuat is another example of the sheng family of China, the sho of Japan and the khaen of Thailand. It is commonly played by the Mhong people in the border area between Vietnam and Cambodia.

The mbuat has a gourd air reservoir which supports six pipes. The pipes are divided into two groups, one of four and the other two. As in the other instruments in this family, the end of the pipe with the free reed is secured inside the gourd wind chest. Each pipe has a finger hole on the side which extends outside the gourd, and sounds when the hole is stopped.

Track 39: "Waking Up" Mbuat. Performed by Dieu Xrot, Dak Nhau Village, Song Be Province, Vietnam. Recorded by Phong Nguyen. 0:29 (125)

Base clarinet played
by Romy Benton

bass clarinet

bamboo is a popular material for construction of musical instruments by musician Romy Benton. The natural density of the interior surface produces a very clear tone; Benton has used this material to create many different sizes and types of aerophones. In this selection the foundation instrument is a clarinet which Benton modifies with the addtion of various shaped bells attached at the end of the bamboo tube. An upward curved bell at the bottom end tends to modify the lower bass notes produced. The direction of the bell can be adjusted toward an audience, or up toward the musician.

A second bell is mounted at the upper end of the clarinet. A hole in the side of the bamboo tube is covered with mylar membrane which adds sympathetic vibrations with the tones produced. (This is similar to the *miriliton* used in African instruments such as the balafon.) A gourd resonator is mounted over this to amplify the effect. The direction of the bell can be turned, either toward an audience, or down facing the musician. Both gourds can be removed for ease of carrying.

Track 40: All gourd saxaphone built and performed by Romy Benton PO Box 10871, Portland, OR 97296 Romy@teleport.com. 0:24 (125)

Matafono found in marketplace in
Montevideo, Uruguay.

matafono

the matafono, in our research, has only been found in a market place in Montevideo, Uruguay. The story told, when this example was purchased, is that this is a slave inspired instrument. The matafono sounds like a kazoo but is without a membrane. The flat gourd is cut in half and thoroughly cleaned. At one end a leather hinge is glued to keep the two halves of the gourd aligned. Through this hinge, a hole ⅜ inch is drilled into the shell, half the hole above the cut line and half the hole below the cut line. On the opposite side another hole, ⅛ inch is drilled through the gourd shell, half above the cut line and half below the cut line.

The player sings or hums into the hole in the leather hinge while holding the gourd closed with one hand. A slight pressure is all that is needed to keep the shell aligned. The air going into the gourd from singing increases the pressure inside the gourd and causes the gourd to separate slightly to relieve the pressure. The rapid, but slight, opening and closing causes the two halve of the shell to vibrate against each other and amplify the sound, resulting in a kazoo like tone.

Track 41: Matafono. A gourd kazoo with no membrane. From Uruguay. Performed by Angel San Pedro del Rio. 0:34 (63)

Kalimbas made and photographed by Matt Collins

kalimba

he kalimba is one of the large family of instruments known as "lamellaphones." The features which they all have in common are a sound board to which are fastened many tines, or tongues, and a resonator to which the sound board may or may not be attached. This instrument is familiar throughout all of Africa in many different forms, which accounts for the many names and traditions which are associated with it.

The kalimba is the style of instrument more familiar in West Africa and subsequently introduced to the West Hemisphere by the slaves, in which the keyboard is permanently attached to a resonator box. The number of keys can range from four to eighteen, but the usual number is eight to twelve. They are usually made of pounded metal, but have also been formed from bamboo or other resilient wood. The tuning varies from tribe to tribe, and the keys can be arranged either from the longest to shortest in a graduated sequence from one end of the soundboard, or with the longest key in the center and the remaining keys alternating side to side with the shortest keys on the outside. The main difference between the kalimba in Africa and those played in the United States is in the tuning. Most western thumb pianos, as they are usually called, are tuned to the eight-note octave. The sound board is permanently attached to the resonator, frequently a half gourd. The resonator may have a hole in the side which may be pulsed by the fingers while playing.

The kalimba is generally played in informal settings, either for individual entertainment or for social gatherings. While other forms of this instrument, such as the mbira, are associated with ritual and tradition, the kalimba is played primarily for enjoyment.

Track 42: "Wind," from *Rhythm Sessions*, Kalimba made and performed by Matt Collins ©1997 Collins Rhythm Craft, 343 Canyon Acres Dr, Laguna Beach, CA 92651 mncollins@hotmail.com, 1:53 (40)

Xavier Quijas Yxayotl (flute) and Guillermo Martinez (water drums) of America Indigena. Photographed in concert at Welburn Gourd Farms, Fallbrook, CA 1999.

music of ancient mexico

this selection, "Corn Dance" by Xavier Quijas Yxayotl incorporates the trilogy of instruments used by the Mayan people in their ceremonies and rituals. The Mayans, as well as many other Indian cultures in North America, felt that music was a specific vehicle for communicating with the spirits. Songs, dances and musical instruments were never played for enjoyment by individuals or small groups. Rather, they were reserved for the very specific purpose of addressing the world of the spirits.

These three groups of instruments played together represent the voice of creation. The drums are of the earth, providing the foundation rhythm for the ritual music, or the heartbeat of the ceremony. The rattle is made of materials of the earth, either from plants, animals, or even insects. The rattle, therefore represents all the living forms that are part of the earth life cycle. The flute creates sound from air, or breath. The flute sounds are the voice of the soul or the spirits themselves.

In this selection, the drums are water drums of three sizes. In contrast to the water drums on track 16, each over tuned bowl has a separate container of water. They are struck by a mallet padded with cornhusk. The rattles, *aya caxtli*, are made of gourds of different sizes, including small dipper and maranka varieties. Typically the rattles of Mayan and other North American cultures all had the noisemakers of seeds or pebbles contained within the shell. Other rattles are made of hollowed turtle shells, dried leather spheres, or even large beetle shells and cocoons.

Several different flutes are played in this piece. Some are constructed of clay and others of gourd, especially the handles of dipper gourds. If the inner surface of the gourd is thoroughly cleaned and coated with a sealant, it will produce brilliant clear tones, such as heard in this selection.

Track 43: "*Danza Del Maiz*" from *Codex—Music of Ancient Mexico*. Gourd water drums, gourd rattles and flutes made by Xavier Quijas Yxayotl. ©1997 Xavier Quijas Yxayotl, America Indigena. 1044 S Gage Ave, Los Angeles CA 90023 5:06 (19)

Guiros, drums, and rattles, made by Opie and Linda O'Brien, Burnt Offerings Studio. Photo by Burnt Offerings Studio. Additional example of traditional guiro from Puerto Rico.

guiro

his is a form of a very popular instrument, which is also known as a *raspa*.

There are versions of this type of instrument in almost every non-European culture, which accounts for the bewildering variety of names associated with it. The common element is a notched surface which can be scraped in rhythmic accompaniment to other instruments, singing or dance. The notched object can be as simple as a stick or bone, which is in turned rubbed by another stick or bone. As used by Native American Indians, the end of the notched stick was set against or inside a hollow resonator, very often a gourd.

The more familiar form of instrument as made and played throughout the Caribbean, Central and South America is made from a hollow container, either a wood box, a hollowed stick or bamboo, or a gourd. (The name 'guiro' is derived from 'guero' meaning gourd.) To play, the musician holds the notched container loosely in one hand, and scrapes the stick back and forth across the notches in rhythmic sequence.

When made from a gourd, the body is thoroughly cleaned and one or more holes are made in the sides to transmit sound. Notches are made along one side with a saw or file. They should not cut completely through the gourd shell, but create indentations so as to form evenly spaced ridges not closer than ¼ inch. The remainder of the gourd is often highly decorated, so that the instrument is made not only to be played, but enjoyed as a work of art.

Track 44: Guiro made and performed by Opie O'Brien, is used on many of the original compositions recorded at Burnt Offerings Studio. To hear more, visit http://www.burntofferings.com. 0:16 (38)

Ektar, gopichand, gubgubbi

lost gourd ensemble

this track features several unusual instrument which are played by the Bauls of Bengal in Northeastern India and Bangladesh. Although the instruments were originally played by wandering mendicants, or religious singers, to accompany themselves in song and dance, they are now being adapted by contemporary music groups intrigued by their haunting sounds.

The 'Ektar,' is a two string drone lute, shaped like a spike fiddle, which provides the drone accompaniment. Its two strings are placed one on top of the other, rather than adjacent to each other, and can be strummed together. The gopichand or gopiyantra has the body of an inverted drum made of a gourd body, to which are attached two legs of a split bamboo fork, whose upper node is left intact. A string extends from a center point in the membrane of the drum resonator, to a tuning peg in the upper portion of the bamboo neck. When the two sides of the bamboo fork are squeezed together, the tension on the string is increased or decreased, and variable pitches are created. The player holds the instrument upright in one hand, squeezing the bamboo legs with the fingers and thumb while plucking the string with the index finger of the same hand.

Another instrument that is commonly used by the Bauls is very similar to the gopichand, but without the bamboo fork framework. Known as the gubgubbi, the inverted gourd drum has a gut string which extends from the center of the membrane, and through the body of the drum, the end of which is secured to a small knob or a cup. The player braces the instrument tight between his chest and elbow, and with the same hand holds the string taut by the wood knob or cup. The string is then plucked by a small pick held in the opposite hand. By varying the tension of the string, many guttural sounds can be created.

The harmonium derives its sound from the free reeds of its sheng ancestor, however, instead of a gourd wind chest, bellows provide the continuous "breath."

Track 45: "The Lost Gourd." ©1998 Jai Uttal. Ektar harmonium, Dotar (miniature sarode), gopichand, gubgubbi, To hear more of Jai Uttal's innovative mix of Eastern and Western musical forms, check out his four CD's on Triloka/Mercury records www.jaiuttal.com 2:35 (103)

(*) Numbers in parenthesis at end of each track description refer to relevant pages in **Making Gourd Musical Instruments**. See below and opposite page for ordering information.

All of the instruments you've heard on the previous 45 tracks can easily be built with a minimum of tools and skill. In fact, the authors have compiled detailed instructions with hundreds of step-by-step photographs for 20 of these instruments in a new book, **Making Gourd Musical Instruments**. In addition to the detailed instructions, forty other instruments from around the world, are photographed and described. In all, this 144 page book contains over 500 full color photographs.

> "... I was amazed at the variety of gourd instruments the world has produced, and over sixty are pictured or described in a clear, straightforward [manner] ... [the] history alone makes the book worth the price ... the raison d'etre of the book is the detailed directions with step-by-step pictures for making twenty instruments from gourds.... This is how-to; written and illustrated at its best." **The Gourd,** the Journal of the American Gourd Society.

> " ... Most of the instruments are simple to make, requiring a minimum of special tools or materials." **Bart Hopkin, Experimental Musical Instruments,** Journal of EMI

> "There is an amazing wealth of information here, covering not only how-to's and history but also extending into the social sciences and even science ... a book that patient crafters will appreciate." **Booklist**

> "Historically, ethnic groups in many countries have used a great number of musical instruments made from gourds. These are legitimate musical instruments made from traditional materials, and they are fully playable as well as being beautifully crafted. Highly recommended for general crafts as well as ethnomusicology collections." **Library Journal**

Call in your order **Toll Free** to 1-800-544-3373 or fax: 1-510-527-7718, or mail to:
The Caning Shop, 926 Gilman Street, Berkeley, CA 94710
http://www.caning.com

QTY	TITLE	PRICE EA.	TOTAL
	Making Gourd Musical Instruments	$27.95	
	The Complete Book of Gourd Craft	$18.95	
	Gourds in Your Garden	$19.95	
	Gourd Crafts—Weekend Crafter	$14.95	
		If in California 7¼% Sales tax	
		Shipping and Handling	$ 4.20
		Total Enclosed	

SHIP TO

NAME

ADDRESS

CITY STATE ZIP

PHONE

PAYMENT CHECK/M.O. VISA MASTERCARD DISCOVER

— — —

CARD NUMBER EXPIRES MONTH / YEAR

ADDRESS ON CARD

NAME ON CARD (PLEASE PRINT) BILLING ADDRESS, IF DIFFERENT

SIGNATURE

The Shop

926 Gilman Street at 8th
Berkeley, CA 94710

Phone: 1.800.544.3373   Fax: 1.510.527-7718
email: gourdmusic@caning.com
http://www.caning.com